CW00481000

Poems of a depressed soul

Emerson S. Rocha

Poems

of a depressed Soul

Preface

In the pages that follow, you will enter a world of intertwined words and emotions, where poetry is the voice of the soul. This book, "Poems of a Depressed Soul," is a profound and intense journey through the complexity of depression, captured in verses that flow like tears and smiles.

As you hold this book in your hands, know that you are not alone. The author, like many of us, faced the darkness of depression at the age of 14. But more importantly, he emerged from that darkness, embracing faith, self-discovery, and the pursuit of joy.

This book is a testament to human resilience, a voice that cries out for everyone to understand that even in the depths of depression, there is hope. You will find poems that explore pain, suffering, and loneliness, but you will also find light, support, and guidance for the journey of self-care.

Before you dive into the following pages, know that here you will find knowledge about depression, guidance on how to overcome it, and poetry that will touch your soul. It is an vitation to recognize that, for everything in e, there is a solution, even for depression.

The message is clear: never allow the ords of others to define your feelings, houghts, and desires. Transform your mind, ansfer only what is good to your heart, and t that positivity reflect in your life.

This is a reminder that self-love is the undation of healing, that God is always by our side, and that you are capable of victory. ive fully, love deeply, and distance yourself om those who cause pain. Discover joy in ie little things and allow yourself to smile, ecause life is a gift.

n the words and emotions of these poems, nay you find not only understanding but also nspiration to face depression with courage nd hope. It is a privilege to share this journey vith you.

Summary

Pain That Doesn't Fade

Can the day arrive without me getting out of bed, searching for a reason in yesterday's tears, 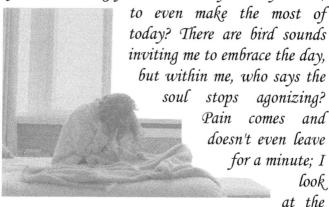 to even make the most of today? There are bird sounds inviting me to embrace the day, but within me, who says the soul stops agonizing? Pain comes and doesn't even leave for a minute; I look at the ceiling from my bed and cry out to God for help. The smile that the night took from me, I wish the day would bring back. I toss and turn in bed, thinking: what am I even going to do? I can sit on the edge of my bed and let rivers of tears flow, or simply close my eyes and try to sleep to see if this pain will go away.

Mother's Embrace

That mother's embrace that tells the pain not to come back, look around, here on Earth, your best friends are your parents. Such a comforting embrace really makes a difference, but it doesn't take away that cursed illness from the soul. For some, it might be another reason to cry a lot, and for others, to be happy for a few seconds, but it takes only a short time for this soul's pain to return and dominate. Can a hug warm you? Yes, it can! But I wish this embrace could put an end to this pain! Can a mother's smile make your heart happy? Perhaps it can! But even if it doesn't bring joy, remember that it's the mother who will be by your side, fighting for you and loving you.

Terrible Ignorance

Why do so many say this is nonsense? If this illness of the soul cruelly and savagely leads so many people to the cemetery, why do some ignore it so much? If the tears don't go away from our faces, why do so many say we're just another poor soul in the world? If the sadness that surrounds us is a "bottomless pit," why do many, in their view, tell us to be calm in our oceans of tears? Without understanding that this is the tearing of our soul, why do some think all of this is nonsense? Setting aside the significant beating and bitterness in the soul, is it necessary to have soul glasses to see all of this? Or does your soul need to be crucified and your heart torn apart to notice 10% of our pains?

Letters of Lost Dreams

If our pain could write, the letters would be made of blood from the cuts that many have endured. They would have sentences written and well underlined, portraying the lives of those who departed with poisoned decisions. It would be a jumble of letters and words with no explanation, hoping for an author to correct paragraphs, line by line, refrain by refrain. And the genre of this story, would it be horror? Never, because not even that genre could depict such pain. The words of pain would have trembling writings, showing the lowest and deepest lows of each life. It would be great if, after so much pain, the ending would be well-deserved smiles, but from this story, there are many final periods of lost dreams.

Breezes of Pain

The depths of a heart that holds the coldness of pain, a heart consumed by this feeling, not even has room for love. If this love were the kind that values me, it could carry all the anguish away in a gentle breeze. Breeze, take the anguish and don't even look back. But when I least expect it, the anguish is by my side because taking it away isn't what the breeze does. Winds that used to flow through a heart full of love, now these winds bring whirlwinds of immense pain.

Sad Dream

I dream of a future where there's no more pain, where a fervent hope comes into our lives, leaving our tears behind, and our smiles become more frequent. This dream, in the comfort of lying down, the sad part is that, with the anguish we're wrapping ourselves in, pain deeply rooted in our soul, the smile came because I called for help. Unfortunately, I fell out of bed, and I woke up from this dream of getting better.

Black and White Gaze

Today, I see in the eyes of many a beautiful brightness filled with color, but looking into my own eyes, I see the black and white of pain. They say that eyes are the mirror of the soul, and I don't see calming answers in that mirror. Stop, eyes, from shedding tears, for now, I'm going to make a decision to 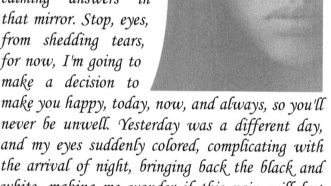 make you happy, today, now, and always, so you'll never be unwell. Yesterday was a different day, and my eyes suddenly colored, complicating with the arrival of night, bringing back the black and white, making me wonder if this pain will last forever.

Peak of Affliction

In the mountain's climb, our aim is the summit, to reach the highest point and leave the tears far below. Climbing with the weight of pain on our shoulders, that indeed can make us fail, giving up on the ascent without even enjoying a beautiful view. If we look up and see how far we have to go, anguish takes over and we may not even move from the ground. On the way up, we hear the voice that the mountain of pain will collapse upon us. Plugging our ears may seem like the solution, but what affects us is that this voice has contaminated the heart. Upon reaching the summit, it's time to throw the rope and celebrate loudly, throwing the rope, it breaks and falls, and now we see the mountain of pain collapsing upon us. The expected rain of torment poured down, thus ending the view from above of the best-earned smile.

Deprived Time

The clock marking the hours as a new day arrives, and here I am, counting milliseconds for my pain to cease, day after day, injuring the soul without restraint, this is no longer life, but rather an engulfing burn. Wanting time to stop might help, time has stopped in pain for many, now we want that to change, to turn  back time and find out why there's so much pain, is it something I did? Do I deserve to have this life without a single happy second? We pause and, looking at the clock, we analyze what it can teach us, and unfortunately, we fail to learn anything except that whether time stops or continues, this pain doesn't want to pass.

Consummation in Pain

Hell with its fire consuming the soul of those who erred so much, this is how the fire of pain coiled around our soul is portrayed, wishing for a bath of good water to extinguish this fire, at least it will disguise the tears rolling down our face. The fury preserves the restlessness of those who once thought of being happy, it screams loudly, frees the soul, will improvement come? Tell me! Tell me! Is there someone willing to hold my hand and rescue me from this pit of darkness? And does salvation come from heaven to save me from the misery of this anguish?

Screams of Torment

The scream of the soul entangled in an inexplicable pain, this pain sits in the heart and stays there, the soul screams and coils in torment, 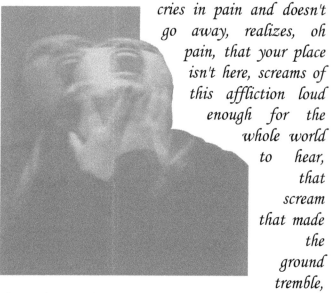 *cries in pain and doesn't go away, realizes, oh pain, that your place isn't here, screams of this affliction loud enough for the whole world to hear, that scream that made the ground tremble, from those who are alive with this pain and from those who died with this pain, screaming was never an option, but it's the portrait of those whose hearts were torn apart by anguish.*

Healing of the Soul

Is there a remedy that can cure this ailment? Is it something bought at the pharmacy or something found within your belief? Arriving at the pharmacy, amidst the multitude of medications, will any of them save this person? Can any medication inject the cure into this soul? A precipice of pain and ruin comes in a full glass, the heart swallows the pain, it's too late, torment is in the veins, circulating from one point to another, making one sicker with each passing day, this anguish that courses through the heart and takes hold of our mind. For every patient, there comes that phrase: "don't give up," but for us, does an injection of joy for the soul like never seen before exist?

Solution for the Soul

Is death the solution to an unexplained pain? Is the shroud of mourning what's missing to complete it all? Or is it the profound sadness of leaving others behind? In this situation, we couldn't care less, for it's in the depths of tears that we've fallen, we've lost the sense of right and wrong, a death of dreams and life, and did it leave its legacy? And worse than this pain is death bringing the suffering I can't help but mention, but the worst is that when this pain strikes at its peak, it's impossible to see, for all we want is to rid ourselves of this pain. I wish to move forward without this pain in my heart, but let's keep in mind that death is not an alternative, and certainly not a solution.

CHeart in Pieces

I need to smile, I need to fight, I need to exercise faith and stop crying, I need my life to have a reason, I need my soul to smile and have faith in my heart, I need to know what to do, I need to piece my heart back together, shard by shard, piece by piece, is it possible to mend this? Is it possible to learn to love myself? I need to put my feet on solid ground and free myself from affliction, I need to 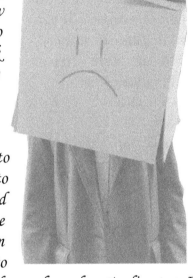 get out of the wreckage of my heart's disaster, I need assurance that I'll see a better day, I need life to embrace me and not let go, and tell me that I will conquer this illness.

Two Terrible Years

It has been two years since I've been suffering here, how much longer will I have to endure this torture, day after day I try to be stronger, but living with this anguish is not life, so much pain is already death, I wish it were two days, two hours, or even two weeks, enough of this pain in my heart, I need my soul to heal from this pain. The fury of this crazy time that wants to take away the best from me, what did I do so wrong that it wants to take my life, second after second I no longer know what to do, but years of affliction turn into nothing, for I no longer want to be at your mercy.

Diving into Trust

Trust is a credit we cannot expect from our soul, this soul that is sinking in despair, thinking, who to trust? If fighting no longer matters to us. Traces of hope may exist internally, buried hopes of those who are no longer here today, mentioning failure should never be a trophy, yet we hope for the glory of victory from this vast sky, the support of a divinity to trust is necessary, and removing the status of a lonely human being from our soul, seeing that our image reflects hope in tomorrow, we should dive into our best trust in that reflection.

Sad Deception

Deception can fail, the deception that life could end this pain, deception emphasizes this pain, if this deception isn't today, will it be me who will go? Deception diverts its target from my heart, it can't hurt this much, that's something unreasonable, destroying the soul can be a cold point without shame, let deception be the intensity of this pain, oh torment, be the deception I never wished, what a terrible deception, for I even deceived myself in this.

Running Away Isn't the Solution

To run away or face the situation, to overcome, heal wounds, to rise from this ground, but where to run? I don't even know, how about running to the end of the street? I got there, and with the pain, I was met. Running away now might be a good option, running into the midst of many, still, my company was the terrible depression. Will it be a beach or the sea, the best place? I got there, and it dragged me deep into pain. Running into the wilderness or a distant island, escape with no result, as what remained was that constant weeping. Places we don't know may be a solution, I wandered, for the pain went along even beyond the coffin.

Horrible Illusion

Can an embrace from someone who loves you so much be an illusion? Someone who fights for your heart with faith, is it truly an illusion to  fight and achieve glory amidst sadness? Illusion amidst sadness is finding victory, deceiving with lies only brings dreadful consequences, claiming that the cure for such pain lies solely in science, searching for something to hold onto, I discovered that it was an illusion that made me sink, do I really have to live without giving my comfort to joy? A dream from another time that now lies dead, we want much more than just happiness; we want to rid ourselves of the discomfort of pain, we want peace, keep false promises at bay, and do not deceive me with the affliction of insults anymore.

How Did I End Up Here?

How did I get into this situation? It feels like just yesterday I lived the best sensation, the sensation of always having joy ready, with that smile from end to end. Now, this horrible feeling has come, day after day, torturing the soul, I need something to calm my mind and something that soothes me, turbulence of pain threatening to lead my life to destruction. What despair, this feeling, I need to get up and move forward, put positivity in my mind, I cannot live far from a healed heart, answer me in a loud voice, how did I end up here?

Hopes on the Ground

I'm dragging, leaving marks of suffering all around, this can't be my purpose, my legacy, I try to get up, move forward without looking back, but with each attempt, the pain comes and knocks me down even more. What a low blow from anguish that I just received, as I no longer see a point in getting up, let alone in living, such a thorny path, I give up on taking the better way, my body and mind no longer know what to do, I've become a doormat of pain, not caring about anything else, lying on the road, letting time roll, the marks I left, dragging these marks don't want to fade, lying here in suffering, such a storm of pain comes, I tried to get up and take another direction, but I took a much stronger fall, something out of the ordinary.

Attachment to Pain

Heart, it's been a long time that it seems like I wake up without you, I get butterflies, a shiver of fear, but I no longer feel like I have you.

Forgive me, heart, I think I've become attached to pain, and I forgot about you, today in my chest, I got used to living in tears, and I no longer feel you, I live with a shattered soul and a broken heart, today, pain is the assured one, and self-love is lost, I've ended this story with pillars of contentment that are no longer mine, today I find myself in the dark, and I bid farewell to the light of joy.

Lost Stories

Ana, who endured so much pain and scars that had no end, Ana, today she's gone, she left in just one moment. Cristiano, his soul still cries out for help, the pain he suffered extends from the older to the younger ones. Worse than Cristiano's scars were the cuts on João's wrists. João tried to be strong, but because of those cuts, João died. Fabiana appeared resolute, to defeat this depression, but to try to eliminate so much pain, Fabiana chose to die. The master of the freedom of life, there's a voice calling you, bring back dear Rosana to life. To what extent do so many need to reach to realize that no matter how much the pain disturbs, the way out is not death? Today was Felipe's day to celebrate another year of life, but on the other side, today, his dear mother weeps. Bring flowers and fragrant roses, leaving as feelings for those embittered lives. Without tears and without a candle, there was the funeral of that suffering lady because when she needed it most, everyone left her alone. Eduardo, in football, every goal he scored made the crowd cheer. He represented his team well, but when he lost his breath of life, there was no one left to revive him. Many are the names of people who have been fighting with this pain, but unfortunately, they died. Let's fight and seek help; we won't add our names to this list, not mine or yours. Let's have faith that one day this internal tormenting pain will disappear. Let's rise and fight, but let's not allow our names to be added to this story.

Damned Pain

Many need to heal their wounds; some turn to drugs, others to alcohol. Is there really a way for my heart? Yes, there is, but alcohol and drugs are not the solutions. Look around you and see the terror that has surrounded you. That's the cause of addiction, in addition to the pain that has engulfed you. The solution that takes so long to arrive, don't delay another second, because I don't know if I can endure it. Solution, why don't you come? I can't stand being a hostage to this pain anymore. The true smile is in the past, it's true, but let's not give up. Let's rise and get out of this state. We have the anguish that hits hard, but let's have faith that a better smile awaits us in the future.

Union

I really want someone by my side who loves me and teaches me how to be loved, someone who reflects their brightness and teaches me to shine. A true, faithful, and loving companion who emerges like the most beautiful flower. Someone by your side to say they will never abandon you, someone who, in a future filled with smiles, makes you believe. But let's not be prisoners of this affliction, please, because the companion who lifts you up also needs to rise from the ground. Let selfishness not rule the heart, because the one who lifts you from the ground deserves more than appreciation. Today, with someone by my side, I feel stronger, capable of fighting and overcoming even death. That person who, with a beautiful smile, brings about the best feeling. Let's live life, and each one will lend a hand.

War for the Soul

If this torture of the soul continues to persist, I don't know if I can bear to be here any longer. Sadness came full of talent, taking away joy, enthusiasm, and my smile, carried away by the wind. Living each day as a lost point in the darkness, clear my soul, make me an inspiration, say yes to life and say no to death. Let it transform tears into smiling days. Let the best of life rule our minds. I entered the war already wounded, and a bomb of pain struck true in my heart. Now, in a dead end, I have to learn to be a warrior, raise the sword, go all in and attack, hold onto life firmly, telling death, "You won't take this life away."

Lost Smile

Today in photos, I saw many smiles that I once lived. Strange, where did I lose so much along the way? Loss doesn't mean it will never return because what's yours, no one will take from you. Torment may come and show the opposite, but that your smile will return, that is clear because we must not forget that among billions, we came into this world to triumph. Even if the chest tears and the pain mistreats the soul, have faith, have patience. It's quite challenging to focus on patience in all of this because an immense amount of pain makes me run from it. My life demands help immediately day after day.

Soul's Game

If all of this is a game, I think I'm doing very poorly. I'm lost, senseless, and not doing well at all. If it's a board game, all my pieces are on the ground, taking with them the defeat of a wounded heart in affliction. Maybe I'm not a good player in this; I've gotten used to many things, but never to such pain. Some force in destiny has checkmated my soul, I need a strategy, a move that will calm me. If to persist in victory, I have to go through this storm, taking the board of pain, I throw it away, and that was my final move.

Blanketed in Pain

If I need faith to resolve all of this, how can I obtain that attribute when even the will to live seems absent? It feels like I'm living in a universe of anguish within me. I don't have faith to put an end to this pain. Opening the window of despair, I feel the need to breathe in some fresh air, but the desire to surrender again to suffering torments me. I no longer know, on this journey, what love is, as the pain surrounding me has become a cloak of bitterness. This cloak is strange, embroidered with pain from thread to thread, and it doesn't remove me from this cold anguish. I try to throw this cloak away when I get up, but when I sit on the edge of the bed, it's only tears that flow, hour after hour.

Soul's Distress

Soul that restrains the best I have to live, a soul clinging to pain, devoid of any desire to flourish. Soul, try at least to detach from this distress, search deep within for the will to find your own redemption. I wanted, soul, to go out and celebrate with you, but today I see that without 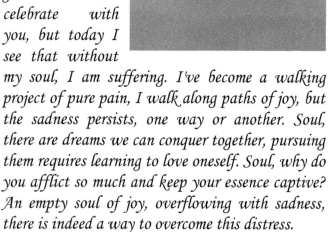 *my soul, I am suffering. I've become a walking project of pure pain, I walk along paths of joy, but the sadness persists, one way or another. Soul, there are dreams we can conquer together, pursuing them requires learning to love oneself. Soul, why do you afflict so much and keep your essence captive? An empty soul of joy, overflowing with sadness, there is indeed a way to overcome this distress.*

Jesus My Comfort

Can loneliness be relieved by company? Perhaps. I try to meditate day after day on the comfort of Psalm 23. I hope from above that a shepherd will come to ease the pain of my soul, that he will be the light of my soul, and that I shall not want. Above all, for my joy to expel anguish away. But I confess that sometimes I want to leave this world, to hide, it may seem crazy, to throw life away with such intense pain. But I ask that you love me, Jesus, and teach me to love myself, my Good Shepherd. If I lose my life, cast it away, and set my dreams aside, my beloved Jesus will be far away. I have to be aware that everything is a choice of yes or no, but I choose to eliminate this pain. Come, Jesus, my help in times of trouble. I want to put an end to this loneliness and the pain that enslaves me, for it's terrible to feel so alone with so many companions by my side.

Bath of anguish

I bathed in waters of anguish that chilled my heart so tight, Flowing streams brought me the worst feelings in the night, Feelings that began so swiftly, now I long to break this chain, From the dirt of this affliction, I must cleanse and heal the pain.

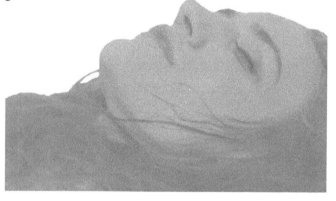

Towards Victory

In an emotional championship, it all began with cheer, but along the journey, anxiety overtook, i fear, bringing with it a confident victory, so near, i won't let depression claim the glory, that's clear.

Obstacle of Life

Jumping over relentless affliction's obstacles, i strove, but one day, i stumbled upon one, and my heart it drove, that's when along this journey, i understood from above, life's obstacles aren't for jumping; we must conquer, prove.

Tranquility

In my life, i seek tranquility to mend the strife, removing the unjust tribulation, the torment of life. I yearn for peace to soothe my weary heart, a loyal joy that will set my soul apart.

Soul's Debt

Accumulating debts of sorrows, a dreadful affliction came to me. Now I'm faced with this bill that seems endless, you see. No matter how i strive to confront this depression within, I'm in a dilemma, unsure how this debt I'll begin to thin.

Letter of Agony

Before sleep, it's always good to offer a prayer, so my dreams may soothe my suffering heart's despair. And in one of these dreams, within my letter of agony, one of the seals was broken, oh, what a tragedy to see.

Territory in depression

In the region of my heart, an entire territory, is gripped by the agony of frustration, a melancholy story. I see no path that could free me from this depression's reign, on the roads I travel, this ailment is a pest, causing endless pain. From north to south, from east to west, its grip won't rest.

Demolition of a Smile

In the construction of my tale, i closely watched the foundation, some missteps along the way led to this deep depression. Now, i must lift my head and witness self-love's reconstruction, yet the fear of tears is taking over, as my smile faces destruction.

Harmonies of Pain

     The notes of my life started in the deepest tone of the note 'C.' Today, the melody that invades my soul has cast my well-being directly into debris. Due to the disheartenment of depression, i can't even harmonize a joyful song. In the sound of this bitterness, i see an entire sonnet play along.

Letters of Lament

Today, i sent letters to my pleasant joy, eagerly awaiting a response if she read them, oh boy. I received the dreadful news that it was anguish who received. And now, disappointed, i linger in this never-ending affliction, deeply aggrieved. Today, a piece of correspondence arrived, of agony and distress, addressed to me, i perceived.

Lost All the Fun

As a complement to our lives, we need some fun, something to distract us, make our hearts overrun. We started this journey with hopes in the beginning, but sadly, I've forgotten the meaning of grinning. The pain in my soul has consumed all in the end, fun, joy, and laughter, no more, my dear friend.

Reflection of Bitterness

Looking in the mirror, i search for a reason to find delight, for depression cruelly stole the essence of joy, taking its flight. Today, the mirror cracked with a dire lack of self-love, my soul reflects in the bitterness, and that's all it's made of.

Gears of Life

In life's machine, i must have lost a cog or two, taking away my finest feelings, bringing wild pain in lieu. I grow disheartened knowing what once moved my zest is slipping away, i must use my best tools: love and faith, to repair life's mechanism, i say.

The Burial of Happiness

Another day passes
with my enthusiasm laid to
rest, now I wander in
solitude on this dark,
winding quest.
Searching for a
glimmer of
optimism in my
past, I strive, but
what can I find in
a joy that's
buried, no
longer alive?

Soul's Virus

Within my genetic code, a trace of contentment I once found, in the quest for profound joy, with afflictions, I was bound. But a viral load of distress was left within my core, And in my DNA, happiness was shattered, forevermore.

Depression from another world

In this vast universe, we don't know if other beings dwell, But the distressing energies around me have a darker tale to tell. Perhaps there are other creatures in this profound cosmic dance, And depression, I believe, is suffering from another realm's expanse.

Mood back to life

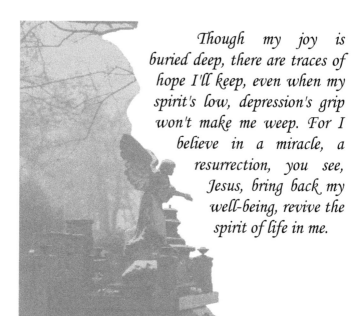

Though my joy is buried deep, there are traces of hope I'll keep, even when my spirit's low, depression's grip won't make me weep. For I believe in a miracle, a resurrection, you see, Jesus, bring back my well-being, revive the spirit of life in me.

Inflamed Heart

In some wounds, the pain's inflammation takes the lead, but the deepest hurts I've felt are the ones my heart did feed. Searching for relief from this exposed wound's cruel dominion, i find no place where the cut has healed, and despair grows like an opinion, and in the face of all this disappointment, my entire soul's inflamed.

Scent of Affliction

The fragrance that once graced my senses with delight, now tainted by the anguish that clings throughout the night. This perfume, once joyful and light in the air, has grown foul as suffering burdens me, unfair. The aroma of happiness that used to linger and play, is now overpowered by a putrid scent of dismay.

Sowing Hope

Today, we sow the seeds for the days ahead, planting smiles, in joy our hearts to be fed. On life's path, a seed of sorrow slipped from our grasp, Today, my soul aches 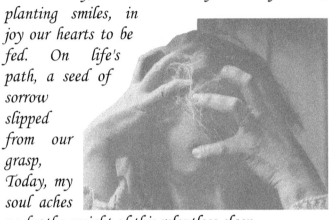 under the weight of this relentless clasp.

Geometry of Pain

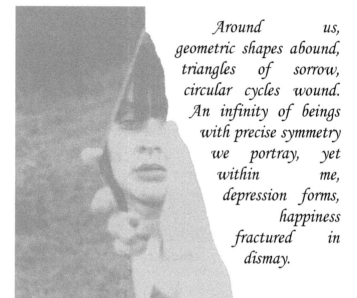

Around   us,
geometric shapes abound,
triangles   of   sorrow,
circular cycles wound.
An infinity of beings
with precise symmetry
we   portray,   yet
within   me,
depression   forms,
happiness
fractured   in
dismay.

Loss of Self-Love

My self-love got lost on the road ahead, now I walk with a heavy heart, hanging my head. Unfortunate it is, this stark reality I bear, the bitterness of my pain shattered my self-care.

Afflicted haunting

Assombrados nós ficamos com aquilo que não conhecemos, mas é no conhecimento que mais e mais crescemos. A depressão, infelizmente, chegou à minha vida bem mais cedo, e por ela não posso morrer, pois esse é o meu maior medo.

Conquering the Fear of Anguish

Enveloped in the discomfort of affliction, here I stand, yearning for the health of my soul, it's what I demand. Sadly, the attachment to the anguish in my life was a deceit, to fight and overcome all this, courage is the treat.

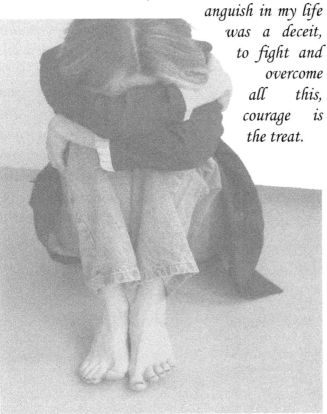

Cruel Reality

This pain that's been tearing my soul apart, it's not mere illusion, it starts by dismantling from within, causing heart's confusion. How to endure this tremendous cruelty, so brutal and severe, the wounds etched on my heart, they are the most intense realities to bear.

The Value of a Smile

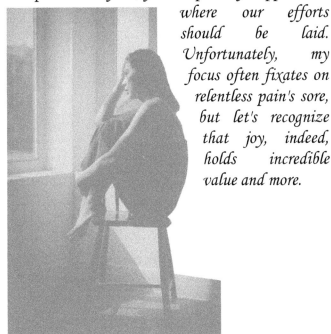

If humor were a currency, we shouldn't let it depreciate or fade, for the price of happiness is where our efforts should be laid. Unfortunately, my focus often fixates on relentless pain's sore, but let's recognize that joy, indeed, holds incredible value and more.

Silencing the Pain

The acoustic sound of soul-piercing pain does persist, constantly playing, invading hearts, and minds it resists. Let's relegate that tune of anguish to a bygone age, trade the acoustic pain for love's digitalized stage.

Garments of Sorrow

I've been donning the sorrow's attire, it doesn't fit, it's true, this unwanted ensemble, I've tried to bid adieu. but this anguish clings to my soul, tight as can be, and now in my very being, it's the perfect fit, you see.

Bewitched depression

This anguish in my soul came in the form of a dreadful spell, enchanting my heart with an agonizing swell, i can't live with this curse any longer, it's true, in my life, this anguish was the worst "enchantment" that I ever knew.

Joy Don't Delay Anymore

If joy is on its way, it's moving at a snail's pace, while discomfort rushed in, a fast and relentless race, in this situation, I ponder what to do, I'll rev up my joy to bring brighter smiles into view.

Depression Isn't a Fairy Tale

I need to find within life's essence appreciation anew, to remove all soul's pain, end the bitterness and the blues. I must restore my self-love and admiration for what's true, to have a happy life with less agony, that's not a fiction, it's the real dues.

Time to Smile

If life's clock loses its hands, I'll be free from affliction's toll, and in my life's story, I'll rediscover love and its role. But even if the hands stay in place, I want all this pain to depart, for my happiness, it's time to restart.

Humbled Heart

My heart has been dragging, shattered and torn, it's been battered and worn, feeling forlorn. I lose faith in the strength to carry on, for this pain has relentlessly humbled my heart.

Attack on my joy

Terrorism in my soul, relentless attack, my shield left aside, there's no turning back. Illusions have shattered my hope, I'm undone, assault on my joy, a painful explosion.

In the Crosshairs of Pain

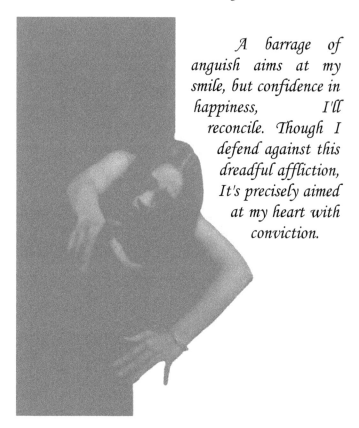

A barrage of anguish aims at my smile, but confidence in happiness, I'll reconcile. Though I defend against this dreadful affliction, It's precisely aimed at my heart with conviction.

Erosion of a Smile

In a journey towards triumph, my love did fall, down a dreadful precipice, it gave its all. Upon reaching the ground, my love was no more, and with every step, my mood, it wore. Down the slope, my smile began to erode, the joy it once held, on this path, it corrode.

Bridge of Pain

Distance has never been a challenge for those who tried, to shorten it with their desires, love as their guide. And in my soul, pain and anguish met on this journey, now, what remains is to destroy the bridge to end the agony.

Thirst for Victory

On a sunny day, my energies deplete and fade away, this is a portrait of my joy, diminishing with each sunray. But in my soul's affliction, i refuse to be defeated, i must share my story, showing the world, undefeated, that i quenched my thirst for victory and succeeded.

Affliction Kinship

Groups are needed to make us feel akin, but in my circle, a mistake i did let in, for within this family, I thought I'd win, yet affliction, neither mother nor kin, has sadly become our next of kin.

Burning Pain in the Soul

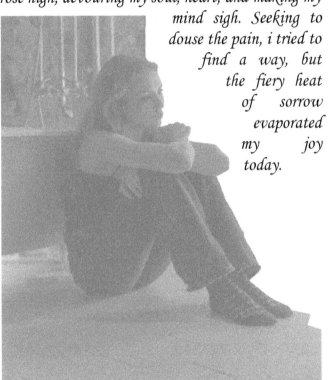

In this scorching heat, fires of affliction rose high, devouring my soul, heart, and making my mind sigh. Seeking to douse the pain, i tried to find a way, but the fiery heat of sorrow evaporated my joy today.

Conversion of Depression

Curses into blessings, a rare transformation takes place, in certain circumstances, it's a path you can embrace. But when it's truly real, let it not fade away, though my soul bears affliction, a curse of another day, it shall transform into my brightest, joyous array.

Communist Oppression of the Soul

In the oppression of my joy, frustration looms so near, bringing anguish, torment, and a world filled with fear, in this current landscape tainted by bitterness and disdain, my smile is subjected to restrictions, such a cruel campaign. But to this depression, I declare with a resolute voice, i'll find happiness, for I'm not living in a joyless choice, amidst constraints, I'll rise, my spirit strong and free, in a world that's not confined by oppressive decree.

Eagle's Vision

In the vision of the future, i sketch paths to joy so clear, for striving toward well-being is a lifelong endeavor i hold dear, with an eagle's sight, i see much farther, reaching new height, i know by persevering, my smile will shine, radiant and bright. Just like an eagle soaring high, i see beyond the horizon's line, and I'll keep the faith, for in this quest, true happiness will be mine, for the journey may be tough, but I will steadfastly persist, in this constant battle for joy, i'll find the happiness that exists.

Votes for a perfect smile

In the party of distress, where anxiety tries to take its toll, i counterattack, determined to mend my wounded soul, though my journey may not be flawless, rest assured it's true, i pledge to you, my perfect smile will ultimately break through. I'll fight against this depression, no matter how tough the strife, with determination in my heart, I'll reclaim my joyful life, in this battle for my well-being, perfection may not be our guide, but I promise you, my smile will be elected, joy by my side.

Suicide Is Not the Solution

The support i lack shouldn't taint my heart with despair, for life itself is our greatest treasure, let's always be aware, even when i feel cornered, pondering an illusion's lure, suicide has never been the answer, of that we can be sure. In the darkest moments when shadows try to hold my hand, let's remember, hope can still rise, like grains of sand, there are lifelines to cling to, friends who care, and love, suicide is not the solution, it's not ordained from above. Our existence is a journey, with pain and joy intertwined, and through life's trials and sorrows, we can heal and find, that suicide, in its deception, promises an end to the pain, but real solutions lie in love, in seeking help, and hope to gain.

Joy in the Palm of Your Hand

Let's take life's water, cleanse our hearts from despair, apply a lathering of joy, let laughter fill the air, with humor held in the palm, scrub away the blue, purify our souls from depression, start life anew. Wash away the stains of sorrow, let happiness flow, turn those frowns into smiles, let your inner radiance show, in the palm of your hand, hold the joy you seek, a heart renewed, a vibrant soul, now life's at its peak.

Showers of Anguish

In this tempest of anguish, i seek shelter to reside, to shield myself with self-love, without which i can't confide, this storm, it tore me from joy, where I once thrived and strived, now I stand here in the rain, with painful drops inside. These showers of anguish, within my soul they pour, i yearn for brighter skies, for peace, and something more, in self-love's embrace, I'll find the strength to soar, and end these showers of anguish, for joy to be restored.

Awaiting a Miracle

In the waiting for a miracle, i stand here, full of hope, eager for my soul's rescue from this painful scope. I long for tranquility, for my heart to smoothly cope, this miracle will release me from the anguish's heavy rope. With bated breath, i wait, my spirit in distress, anticipating the moment when my heart finds redress, i pray for solace to come, my soul to convalesce, in this miracle's embrace, my pain will be much less.

Painful Dates in Time

Turning the pages of time, i watch as days come and go, despite the passing moments, this anguish within still grows. Yet, i realize i must tear away pages of frustration, though, in life's calendar, I can't 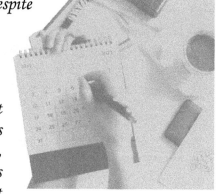 see the moment this pain will go. Days come and go, as relentless as the tide, but this lingering sorrow within me won't subside. In the chronicles of life, i seek a place to hide, hoping that one day, this pain will finally divide.

Pain control

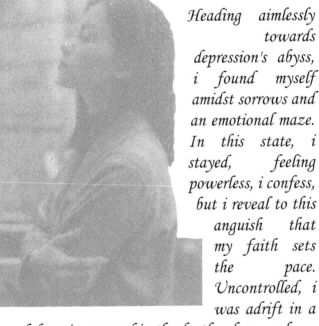

Heading aimlessly towards depression's abyss, i found myself amidst sorrows and an emotional maze. In this state, i stayed, feeling powerless, i confess, but i reveal to this anguish that my faith sets the pace. Uncontrolled, i was adrift in a sea of despair, trapped in the depths of my soul, my heart laid bare. Yet, I'll show this affliction, I'll make it aware, that my faith guides my path, my soul's welfare i declare.

Jesus solution to any Problem

In times of depression, for our healing's ignition, we need a remedy, not just idle submission. Let's not leave our souls adrift in the tempest's condition, for even as this poem nears its final rendition, remember, dear friend, there's one constant prescription, with Jesus as our guide, there's no contradiction. He's the answer to all, the ultimate elixir's fruition, so keep him as your priority, your soul's true foundation.

Postscript

Dear Reader,

As you've reached the end of this book, I hope you've experienced a journey of reflection, emotion, and discovery. The poems you've read capture the intricacies of life, the highs and lows, the joys and sorrows, in a way only poetry can.

Through the words of these poems, the author invites us to explore the deepest corners of the human soul. They remind us that life is a journey filled with challenges, but also moments of beauty and hope. It's a journey we all share, despite our differences in individual experiences.

Poetry has the power to connect us with our own emotions and the experiences of others. It invites us to contemplate, question, and feel. The poems in this book bear witness to human resilience and the pursuit of light, even in the darkest of circumstances.

As you close this book, I hope you take with you not only the words and images you've found here but also a sense of connection, empathy, and inspiration. May these poems accompany you on *your own journey, reminding you that even in the toughest hours, there is always room for hope and healing.*

I thank you for sharing this moment of reflection with me. May this work continue to inspire you to explore the depths of the human experience and find beauty in the imperfections of life.

With gratitude,

Emerson S. Rocha.

Connect With Us

Did you enjoy the E-book "Poems of a Depressed Soul"? Keep following us to stay up to date with the latest news, exclusive tips, and inspirational content! Follow us on social media so you don't miss anything. Together, we can explore a world of knowledge and creativity!

Help us on our social media by following and supporting our work. Our social media profiles are new, and we are starting projects and work aimed at all kinds of audiences. Thank you in advance to everyone.

@autoresrocha   @autoresrocha   autoresrocha   @autoresrocha

Milton Keynes UK
Ingram Content Group UK Ltd.
UKHW020652201123
432908UK00019B/2324